I'M SAVED! Now What?

I'm Saved!
Now What?

Tanicka Heiskell

XULON PRESS

Xulon Press
2301 Lucien Way #415
Maitland, FL 32751
407.339.4217
www.xulonpress.com

© 2020 by Tanicka Heiskell

All rights reserved solely by the author. The author guarantees all contents are original and do not infringe upon the legal rights of any other person or work. No part of this book may be reproduced in any form without the permission of the author. The views expressed in this book are not necessarily those of the publisher.

Unless otherwise indicated, Scripture quotations taken from the King James Version (KJV) – *public domain*.

Scripture quotations taken from the Holy Bible, New Living Translation (NLT). Copyright ©1996, 2004, 2007 by Tyndale House Foundation. Used by permission of Tyndale House Publishers, Inc.

Scripture quotations taken from the English Standard Version (ESV). Copyright © 2001 by Crossway, a publishing ministry of Good News Publishers. Used by permission. All rights reserved.

Scripture quotations taken from the Holy Bible, New International Version (NIV). Copyright © 1973, 1978, 1984, 2011 by Biblica, Inc.™. Used by permission. All rights reserved.

Scripture quotations taken from the Amplified Bible (AMP). Copyright © 1954, 1958, 1962, 1964, 1965, 1987 by The Lockman Foundation. Used by permission. All rights reserved. Printed in the United States of America.

ISBN-13: 978-1-5456-8101-5

Table of Contents

Acknowledgements ix

Introduction xi

Chapter 1: The Make-up of Man 1

Chapter 2: What Took Place? 15

Chapter 3: Holy Spirit 27

Chapter 4: Building and Maintaining Your Relationship 33

Chapter 5: A New Life 41

Prayer of Salvation 59

Additional Resources to Read for Spiritual Growth 61

Acknowledgements:

First, I must acknowledge the presence, power, grace, and love of my Heavenly Father. It is by His Spirit that I was able to complete this book. Father, I pray that it brings You glory and draws us closer to You. To my spiritual parents, Bishop Daniel Robertson Jr. and Co-Pastor Elena Robertson: Your leadership and teachings helped me to develop into the person I am today. I am so thankful God allowed me to be connected to you, and I am grateful for every lesson learned and how I've grown spiritually because of your example. I want to thank my family: my mother, Joyce, and my children, Keith, Kavon, Tory, and Tremere. I thank you for supporting me and for believing in me. I love you all so much. To my family, natural and spiritual: Each one of my Mt. Gilead elders, overseers, brothers, and sisters who prayed for me regarding this vision, thank you for every word of encouragement throughout this process. I thank you. I'm saved! Now what?

Introduction

Have you ever asked, "Now what?" I am almost sure that at some point in this life, we have all come to ask that question. I have asked that question many times, and I still often find myself asking that same question even today, as it pertains to certain situations that may arise in my life. There is one question that I'd like to address in this book, and that question is "I'm saved. Now what?" I believe that with the guidance of the Holy Spirit, we will be able to see "now what."

Let me take you back for a little while. Saved at an early age, I grew up and found myself asking, "What do I do now?" I wasn't trained or taught about the importance of having a real relationship with God. I viewed and understood God as a distant being who lived in heaven, and if I lived right, I would one day go to heaven to live with Him. My perception was that I needed to act a certain way because if I didn't, then God would be mad at me. So, for years, I had a wrong concept of God, and I didn't have a personal relationship with Him, although I thought I was ok. Looking back now, I am so thankful for His love for me and the people He has placed in my life. They are helping me to see how to have a real relationship with God, and the more I learn of Him, the more I realize how much He loves me and who I am in Him. I will forever be learning about Him, and what a great place to be.

Since starting this journey, I have learned God is a loving God and Father.

1 John 4:7-8

> *Beloved, let us love one another: for love is of God, and every one that loveth is born of God, and knoweth God.*

Introduction

He that loveth not knoweth not God; for God is love.

    The mere human language can't describe God in all His splendor, majesty, and glory. I may never really know all that there is to know about Him; however, He makes it possible for us to get to know Him personally. We can be sure that He loves us and that He has made a way for not only me, but for all of us to become His sons and daughters.

    I gave my life to Jesus when I was a young girl, and even during that, I honestly didn't understand all that took place during that spiritual transaction. I knew I was giving my life to Jesus, and I believe that He died for my sins and God raised Him from the dead on the third day. I wanted Him to be Lord over my life, but I didn't understand the depth of what was taking place at that time. As a result, for years, I felt that there was more, but I didn't know how to get to that "more."

    It wasn't until my late twenties that I sought to know God and Jesus on a deeper level.

Now, this seeking didn't happen until life had already started to beat me up. Nothing was working in my life, and I didn't like the person I had become. I had become a teen mother, I had been in unhealthy relationships, and I was making bad choices. After all, I was saved, but I was still doing my own thing. I was not living from God. I would go out and "do me" all week long and then go to church on Sunday morning. I would religiously "go to church" as a routine, but not "be the church" to those around me. I didn't have a deep understanding of God's will or His purpose for my life; I didn't have a relationship with Him, nor did I have one with Jesus.

At that time in my life, my interaction with God consisted of praying now and then when I needed something or listening to gospel music to make myself feel better. However, I never took the time to find out what He required of me or to understand His thoughts toward me. I never sat still to hear His voice or to inquire of Him, never inviting or recognizing His presence. I didn't know it was possible

Introduction

to have that type of relationship with Him. I needed a change, a real change.

I remember this like it was yesterday; I had nowhere to go and no one to turn to, so I thought, but God was there. I felt like I was a failure. I remember crying out to God for help. I couldn't see it then, but in spite of my view of God, up to this point in my life, He never gave up on me. He never stopped loving me, despite all of my mistakes. I see now He was always there (Ps. 139:7-8). I knew one thing: God was the only person who could help me out of my current situation. Shortly after I rededicated my life back to the Lord Jesus, I began to seek after Him the best way I knew how. I remember growing up seeing my aunt read the Word and listening to teachings from well-known television pastors, so I started there. Let me say this: Not all the experiences and the things I saw or learned were completely wrong. God used various people to help me know that He is real.

Let me also clear up another misconception. Many people think that when you come to

Jesus, your actions will be perfect and you won't ever make another mistake in your life. This is not true because our souls aren't saved; they have to be renewed. But I will talk more about that later. In my seeking, have I done everything right? Have I missed the mark since then? Yes, and God knew what I would do. I sincerely repented (had a change of mind), and I sought His help. I kept going; I "got back in the race."

I've learned that when you miss the mark, make a mistake, and are simply doing what you know how to do to live rather than practicing sin (according to Matt. 6:33, KJV), you mustn't hide from the Father. Come to Him; be real and honest with Him and yourself. Have a repentant heart and receive forgiveness through the blood of Jesus. Keep seeking Him, learning more about Him and who you are in Him, and you will be on your way. I wanted to share this because too often, after we do something or miss the mark, we get stuck and spend days, weeks, or even years afraid to confess that shortcoming to God. 1

Introduction

John 1:9 (KJV) asks how can we hide from the one who knows all?

James 4:8 (KJV)

> Draw near to God and He will draw near to you. Cleanse your hands, you sinners, and purify your hearts, you double-minded.

As I sought the ways of the Lord, He began to reveal to me who He is and my identity. He was building my foundation. I remember visiting a church, and although I kept trying to join, no one ever called me back. At that time, I didn't understand why, but my Father knew. I see now I was there to learn some things but not to join that church. I kept seeking, and in my seeking, I would spend a lot of time listening to messages from Dr. Creflo Dollar and Kenneth Copeland because I wanted to be taught. I wanted to get to know God, but I didn't know much about the Holy Spirit at that time; however, I knew and believed that Jesus saves. I was searching for someone to teach me how to live my new life in Christ Jesus. God was ordering my steps (Ps. 37:23, KJV).

One day, I was listening to the Word on TV, and a well-known man of God said to pray and ask God to show you the church He has for you. So, I did just that. I prayed, and God ordered my steps to Mt. Gilead Full Gospel International Ministries through a recommendation from a friend and co-worker. This was a significant turning point in my life and for my family. If I recall correctly, I visited about two or three times before joining the church. I just knew. So, now I am encouraging you to do the same; pray and ask God to show you the church home He has for you.

You must get connected to the man and woman of God (not just anyone) assigned to your life. Without my connection to my spiritual parents, Bishop Daniel Robertson Jr. and Co-Pastor Elena Robertson, I would not be the person I am today. Nor would I be on the path that is preordained for my life. I am so thankful for the power of connection. Through my connection with them, my spiritual parents have taught me the importance of having a real relationship, with honor and respect, for God. They taught me how to manifest the Word. They showed me how to meditate on the Word of God, praying daily, and they are continually teaching me about my true identity in Christ and how to walk with God. Most importantly, to me, they are the living examples of the very life I was desperately searching for all those years ago; they are helping me to now live out my new life in Christ Jesus.

Hebrews 6:12 (NLT)

> *Then you will not become spiritually dull and indifferent instead you will follow the example of those who are going to inherit God's promise because of their faith and endurance.*

In years past, I've heard many people say just get saved, and that's it. No, that is not it. Getting saved is just the beginning. Being saved is extremely important because it is the doorway. Jesus is "the way" to this life with God and is required, but it is not the end; it is just the beginning. This life is a new way of living; it's an opportunity to partner with God to live out your original purpose. God has set this life up for you, and He is ready to take you on this preordained journey. My prayer to the Father is that He uses this book to draw you into a closer relationship with Him and His will for your life; to help guide and lead you into your place of dominion and authority in Him.

Chapter 1

The Make-up of Man

1 Thessalonians 5:23 (ESV)

> Now may the God of peace Himself sanctify you completely and may your <u>whole spirit</u> and <u>soul</u> and <u>body</u> be kept blameless at the coming of our Lord Jesus Christ.

I want to take this time to explain the make-up of man. What makes up a man or a woman? When I started understanding more about who I was, I didn't understand that I was a spirit; I have a soul, and I live in a body. I operated only from my natural senses, so I knew about the body because it was obvious I could see that. I knew of the soul (my mind, will, and emotions), but I had no real concept of how to control my soul or the importance of my spirit. Man has three parts: the spirit, the soul, and the body. The Trinity is God the Father, the Son, and the Holy Spirit.

You Are a Spirit

We are spirit beings. 1 Thessalonians 5:23 mentions the full make-up of man. It states that your whole spirit, soul, and body must be kept blameless. In Genesis 1:26, God said, "Let us make mankind in our image, in our likeness."

John 4:24 (KJV)

God is a Spirit: and they that worship Him must worship Him in spirit and in truth.

The image God created us after was His Spirit.

Your spirit is unseen to this natural world, unlike your body. When you became saved, your spirit becomes born again; God comes to dwell on the inside of you in your Spirit man.

John 3:1-18 (KJV)

> *John 3 is the account of Jesus explaining to Nicodemus (a Pharisee a member of the Jewish ruling council) regarding what being born again is.*

Your spirit is now perfect, and it carries the glory of God. Your spirit believes and agrees with only the Word of God. As a born-again believer, we are to be led by the Spirit.

We are to feed our souls the Word of God so that it can agree with our spirits. When the two are in perfect alignment, then we can understand what is coming from the Spirit. It will require yielding and obedience to what is transferred from our spirits to our souls. To be a victorious child of God, we must learn how to yield and flow with the Spirit of God that is leading us.

Your Soul

Your soul is made up of your mind, will, and emotions, as a very brief explanation. It also includes your intellect, imagination, and reasoning. It's your thinker, how you think; your feeler, how you feel about certain things; and your chooser, how you make choices. At the new birth (a spiritual rebirth, when the human spirit is born again by the Holy Spirit when Christ is accepted), your soul was not born again, nor was it automatically recreated like your spirit man. In Romans 12:2, the Word of God teaches us to not be conformed but transformed by the renewing of our minds (soul). Let God transform you into a new person by changing the way you think.

Since birth, people, situations, and circumstances have conformed us to the customs, ways, and thought patterns of this world, especially being told how to think and how to feel toward certain situations. In most cases, these things weren't based on the principles of God's Word but instead were created from the opinions of others. The renewing of the mind will take effort on your part, and the Word of God must be used to renew the mind.

The word "renew" means to resume after an interruption or to re-establish (a relationship). The process of renewing the mind is placing our minds back into their original state of communing with God and/or thinking the way God intended for us to think before the fall of the First Adam (Gen. 3).

Renewing your mind to line up with your Spirit, the Word, and the ways of God is a vital necessity to walk out your new life in Christ Jesus. The process of renewing your mind or soul is going to take help from the Holy Spirit and a desire to know Him on your part. Initially, your soul is not going to want to do this on its own, and I have learned no one will be able to do this for you. It is a choice you will have to make and apply your will to in order to remain committed to taking control of your soul and causing it to submit in its proper order, which is under your spirit man.

The soul is to be trained with the Word of God. To tame and train the soul requires help from the Holy Spirit, your will, faith, and the Word. For me, it also helped to see my spiritual leaders, brothers, and sisters manifest the Word. Seeing and hearing their testimonies helped me to believe that I could walk out God's Word as well.

To grow up in Christ, renewing the mind must be a priority. This is done by taking the Word of God to help you see yourself and by meditating on the Scriptures and through prayer. Ask the Holy Spirit to open the Scriptures and to give you understanding. When you do, the Spirit of God (Holy Spirit) will begin to reveal to you your identity and the Father's ways and will. You may get promptings; I like to call these promptings the leading of the Holy Spirit. But to yield to these promptings, your thinking and will must be renewed and submitted under your spirit man.

Let me take a few minutes to explain meditation. Meditation, as defined in the KJV Dictionary:

To dwell on anything in thought; to contemplate; to study; to turn or revolve any subject in the mind;

To intend; to have in contemplation.

To think on; to revolve in the mind.

I believe it is possible to think about something so much that you began to experience what you have been thinking. My bishop has said many times that "manifestation begins in the mind."

Meditation is so important; you can, on purpose, meditate on things that line up with the Word of God, or you can have negative reflection and listen to lies that the enemy speaks to you. These lies go against the will and Word of God for your life. What you meditate on and think about is your choice. You can choose to meditate on the will of God and believe His word concerning your life (the truth), or you can meditate on the lies that don't line up with His Word and never experience

God's best. Either way, you will see the fruit of that thought.

Renewing the mind will take time because a lot of wrong thinking (thinking that doesn't line up with the Word) will have to be undone in you. For me, the old mindset always tries to take over my thoughts, even now; however, I am getting better at identifying those thoughts and conversations with myself that try to creep in. I am so glad that the Word teaches us what to do with those thoughts that don't line up with the Word.

2 Corinthians 10:5

> *Casting down imaginations, and every high thing that exalteth itself against the knowledge of God, and bringing into captivity every thought to the obedience of Christ;*

> *So, when a thought comes that says you are a failure, you must choose the right response and say, "Oh, I take that*

thought captive because that doesn't line up with what God's Word says about me. The Scripture says that I am more than a conqueror through Him who loved me (Rom. 8:37). I choose to believe God's Word about me, not that lie."

The more you practice recognizing those thoughts and ponder on what you are thinking about, the more you will realize your thoughts for what they are. You can then correct anything that is not in line with the Word. God is so faithful; He has given us so many tools to use. If there is ever any question about what to do with your thoughts, the answer can be found in:

Philippians 4:8 (KJV)

> *Finally, brethren, whatsoever things are true, whatsoever things are honest, whatsoever things are just, whatsoever things are pure, whatsoever things are lovely, whatsoever things are good*

report; if there be any virtue, and if there be any praise, think on these things.

The Word of God takes the guesswork out of life. God places people in our lives that can speak into our lives. We can follow and learn from them, and with the help of the Holy Spirit, we can monitor our thoughts and renew our minds. All of these things are training our souls.

The Body

All of us live in a body; the body is needed to operate in this physical world. Your body is what you see when you look in the physical mirror, with the natural eye. It is the house you live in to operate in this world legally. Our Lord and Savior, Jesus, needed a physical body to work in this earth. Your physical body believes the five senses (see, hear, taste, smell, and touch): it does what the mind tells it to do. Your body needs real food, and it requires exercise to remain healthy.

How They Work Together

Your spirit is perfect. The spirit believes the Word of God and is loaded with everything you will need that pertains to life and godliness. The mind (soul) requires the Word of God. The body does what the mind says.

When first starting as a new, born-again believer, I like to say that we begin as babes. The Bible talks about being fed with milk.

1 Peter 2:2

As newborn babe, desire the sincere milk of the word that they may grow thereby:

Continuing in the Word, and being trained by your spiritual leaders, you will then begin to grow and become ready for solid food; this is still the Word of God. You will be walking in more maturity and skilled in the Word. Know how to manifest what the Scripture says, and walk and flow with God and in your identity. They that know their God shall be strong and do exploits.

Hebrews 5:14 (NLT)

Solid food is for those who are mature, who through training have the skill to recognize the difference between right and wrong.

There is continuous development in growing in the ways and will of God and learning how to operate from your identity. Your spiritual leaders will help teach you the Word and the ways of God. They will help you to grow up and mature in the things of God. Now, I want to say that it is not all dependent on spiritual leaders; you to have to take responsibility for your growth and development. We are not only to hear the Word but to be doers of the Word. This requires faith and action on your part.

I used to think that if I just come to church every Sunday, then what is being taught will automatically happen in my life. If there is a real anointing, some change will happen; it will give you the desire for change, but true change is going to require your participation. The Word says, "For as the body without the spirit is dead, so faith without works is dead also" (James 2:26, KJV). We have to apply what we receive from our connection, those that we follow, trust, honor, and respect. We are going to have to use our faith and put some legs or action with our faith to see the manifestations of God's Word and perfect will in our lives happen. All parts of your being are going to have to come inline.

To break this all down, your spirit believes the Word of God; your soul believes your thoughts, will, and emotions (right thinking will come from spending time in and with the Word); and your body does what your mind tells it. Each one of these parts is made to work together, and they must work in the proper order so you can receive and correspond appropriately to the promises of God. The appropriate order is spirit first, soul, and then body.

Chapter 2

―――∝―――

What Took Place?

Proverbs 4:7 (KJV)

Wisdom is the principal thing; therefore get wisdom: and with all your getting get understanding.

Ephesians 2:8 (KJV)

For by grace are ye saved through faith; and that not of yourself; it is the gift of God:

In all your getting, get understanding. We must know and understand what took place during salvation. I pray that revelation knowledge will continue to flow and that all Jesus is and what He did for us will be revealed as we live out our new lives in Him. Jesus delivered us from the curse and gave us benefits that He purchased for us through the finished work on the cross. Through Christ, we have a salvation package. Jesus saved us from any and everything that would try to keep us from knowing who we are. Jesus, through His love and sacrifice, has placed us back in right standing with God. Your original position is restored.

Jesus can't be left out of our "now what", He is the reason for our "now what." Jesus must be at the center of your relationship with God the Father; after all, Jesus is the reason why we're reconciled back to God and the place of righteousness, which was done by the finished work on the cross.

He delivered you from all oppression and depression that would try to keep you separated from God. As we talked before, the soul will have to be renewed, and this is a process; however, the Word tells us we have the mind of Christ, so it is possible to have the mind of Christ. He has blessed our finances and every area of life. Jesus didn't leave anything out according to the will of God.

John 10:10 (KJV)

> *The thief cometh not, but to steal, and to kill, and to destroy. I am come that they might have life, and that they might have it more abundantly.*

Jesus came to show us who we are in Him. IT IS FINISHED!

The question we must personally answer is will we accept all of the benefits and walk them out?

Let us take a look back at the book of Genesis, when God created human beings.

Genesis 1:27-28; 31 (NLT)

> *So God created human beings[a] in his own image.*

In the image of God he created them; male and female he created them.

Then God blessed them and said, "Be fruitful and multiply. Fill the earth and govern it. Reign over the fish in the sea, the birds in the sky, and all the animals that scurry along the ground."

Then God looked over all he had made, and he saw that it was very good!

And evening passed and morning came, marking the sixth day.

We can see God and man's relationship on display. He also gave man the authority to govern the earth. If we read further, we can see God cared for man so much that He didn't want him to be alone (Gen. 2:21-25).

Since God created them, He knew everything about them. He was pleased with what He had made.

Then they, Adam and Eve, were tempted by the evil one, and they fell through disobedience, giving up their authority to the evil one.

I believe their disobedience to God and obedience to the evil one hurt God, and there had to be a consequence for the sin. I also believe God loved them so much that He set some things up to protect them (Gen. 3:22-24), such as making them clothes (Gen. 3:21). He didn't just throw them away. That's real love.

As a result of Adam and Eve's sin against God, they were no longer in their original state of purity.

A sin nature entered in, and because of this sin nature, we needed an all-loving Savior to pay the price for the sin and to put us back into right standing with God. Jesus made it possible for us to now be reconciled back to God and to have eternal life. We could not pay the price; only through the spotless, shed blood of Jesus the Christ would this be possible. No other way could or would do.

As we read through the Old Testament, we see where animal sacrifices were made once a year for the people's sin. The priest was the only one who could make the sacrifice for the people's sins each year.

Jesus is our High Priest who was worthy of being the sacrifice for our sin once and for all. He completed this when He was crucified on the cross. God loves us so much that He didn't allow us to be separated from Him.

John 3:16

> *For God so loved the world, that He gave His only begotten Son, that whosoever believed in Him should not perish, but have everlasting life.*

John 3:17

> *For God sent not his Son into the world to condemn the world; but that the world through Him might be saved.*

So, He sent His best, His Son, Jesus, to pay the price for our sin. God is a just and righteous God, and there had to be payment for sin. Although Jesus was not guilty of anything, He said, "I'll go in their place; I'll go and pay the price for (say your name)." I want you to stop and think about this: an innocent man laid down His life for all, knowing that some would not accept Him, but many have and will.

The cross was a gruesome death, and the Scriptures describe Jesus being beaten so severely that you could not recognize what manner of man He was. Real love in action drove His obedience, even unto death. His actions showed how much He loves us, that He would lay down His life for a friend.

John 15:13 (KJV)

Greater love hath no man than this, that a man lay down His life for His friends.

2 Corinthians 5:21 (KJV)

For He hath made Him to be sin for us, who knew no sin; that we might be made the righteousness of God in Him.

Jesus came to seek and save that which was lost. He lived, was beaten, hung, bled, and died on the cross for you and me. He took the punishment and wore the curse so that we can have back the blessing and be reconciled to the Father. That's not all: He Is Risen!

Galatians 3:13 (NLT)

But Christ has rescued us from the curse pronounced by the law. When He was hung on the cross, He took upon Himself the curse for our wrongdoing. For it is written in the Scriptures, "Cursed is everyone who is hung on a tree."

Isaiah 53:5 (NKJV)

> *But He was wounded[a] for our transgressions, He was [b]bruised for our iniquities; The chastisement for our peace was upon Him, And by His stripes[c] we are healed.*

Luke 24:5-7 (NKJV)

> *Then, as they were afraid and bowed their faces to the earth, they said to them, Why do you seek the living among the dead?*
>
> *He is not here, but is risen! Remember how He spoke to you when He was still in Galilee,*
>
> *Saying, The Son of Man must be delivered into the hands of sinful men, and be crucified, and the third day rise again.*

The Gospel is the good news about what Jesus did through the finished work on the cross, the good news of being reconciled back to the Father.

Romans 10:9 (NLT)

If you openly declare that Jesus is Lord and believe in your heart that God raised him from the dead, you will be saved.

Ephesians 2:8-10 (NLT)

God saved you by his grace when you believed. And you can't take credit for this; it is a gift from God.

Salvation is not a reward for the good things we have done, so none of us can boast about it.

For we are God's masterpiece. He has created us anew in Christ Jesus, so we can do the good things he planned for us long ago.

When Jesus was raised up, He rose with all power and authority, and He defeated death, hell, and the grave. He took the curse and gave us the blessing. He took the keys. He has given you the same power and authority.

Luke 10:19 (KJV)

Behold, I give unto you power to tread on serpents and scorpions, and over all the power of the enemy; and nothing shall by any means hurt you.

Matthew 16:19 (NLT)

And I will give you the keys of the Kingdom of Heaven. Whatever you forbid on earth will be forbidden in heaven, and whatever you permit on earth will be permitted in heaven.

John 11:25 (NLT)

> *Jesus told her, "I Am the resurrection and the life. Anyone who believes in me will live, even after dying."*

Ephesians 1:11 (NLT)

> *Furthermore, because we are united with Christ, we have received an inheritance from God, for He chose us in advance, and He makes everything work out according to His plan.*

Chapter 3

Holy Spirit

I write about the Holy Spirit with honor, reverent fear, and trembling because I do not want to misrepresent the Spirit of God in any way. The Holy Spirit is a person; He is the Spirit of God. There is God the Father, God the Son, and God the Holy Spirit. They are one. When you become born again, you received a measure of the Holy Spirit at that time during salvation.

Jesus prayed to the Father that He would give you another comforter so that He may abide with you forever. I believe there are levels to the Holy Spirit that we can access; it's dependent on how much we acknowledge Him and how much access we give Him to operate in our lives.

John 14:16 (AMP)

And I will ask the Father, and He will give you another Helper (Comforter, Advocate, Intercessor, Counselor, Strengthener, and Standby) to be with you forever.

We are never alone. God has given us His Spirit, who operates in the earth through us. I have learned for this to happen we must learn to yield and flow with the Holy Spirit.

I will tell you that in my personal life, I have had to crucify my flesh every day so that I can flow with the Spirit of God. I have this thing about always wanting to be in control. I always wanted to be in the know and had to figure out all the details, although I didn't realize this was what I was doing. Even today, I am still learning how to consistently flow with the Holy Spirit. It requires faith and trust, and we must learn how to flow, even without all of the details.

Every moment, I have to purposely practice acknowledging the Spirit and knowing that I need His help with everything. There are so many times when I've missed the leading of the Holy Spirit. I put my soul ahead of my spirit, and I didn't surrender and submit my will to His.

We all must learn to keep our souls in check because our souls will try to keep us from getting closer to God. What keeps me going is the Word. It teaches me that the work God has begun in me, He will complete.

Philippians 1:6 (NLT)

> *And I am certain that God, who began the good work within you, will continue his work until it is finally finished on the day when Christ Jesus returns.*

I want to share with you one significant gift that is available to you, now that you are saved and a born-again child of God. I did not know about this gift, nor did I receive this gift until I visited Mt. Gilead Full Gospel International Ministries, the church that God has connected me to now. I am not saying that you have to wait for God to lead you to a church to receive the baptism of the Holy Spirit; this gift is available to you now. I learned the Holy Spirit is a gift from God, with the evidence of speaking in tongues (a language unknown to your natural senses). Receiving the gift of the Holy Spirit allows us to walk in a more significant measure of what Jesus has done for us.

I recall the invitation was given, and I knew that I hadn't had the baptism. I also knew I wanted everything that God had given to me, so I went up to the altar to receive. Receiving the gift of the Holy Spirit is for you, and it is still available today; the only requirement is that you need to be born again.

When receiving the Holy Spirit, you can't comprehend Him with your mind; this is a spiritual transaction and a gift that must be received by faith. So, if you try to think about "how" this is going to happen, then you may have a hard time receiving; however, I pray that it will be easy for you. Just use your faith to receive, just as you did when you received the gift of salvation.

Acts 2 gives an account of being filled with the Spirit of God. When you speak, it will be in a language that you will not understand. There are other gifts the Holy Spirit gives as He wills, but I am not talking about those gifts at this time.

When you pray in your heavenly language, it is a perfect prayer unto God.

1 Corinthians 14:2 (NLT)

For if you have the ability to speak in tongues, you will be talking only to God, and people won't understand you. You will be speaking by the power of the Spirit but it will all be mysterious.

Jude 1:20 (NKJV)

But you, beloved, building yourselves up on your most holy faith, praying in the Holy Spirit.

Praying in the Spirit is a perfect prayer unto God. Our perfect prayer language comes with so many benefits; it is supernatural. Praying in the Spirit will help with hearing His voice, as well as understanding the Word and promptings. I believe there is so much more that happens in the Spirit. I want to encourage you to be filled with the baptism in the Holy Spirit.

Chapter 4

Building and Maintaining Your Relationship

Matthew 6:33 (NIV)

But seek first His Kingdom and His righteousness, and all these things will be given to you also.

Your new life begins with building and maintaining your personal relationship with the Father, the Son, and the Holy Spirit. Your relationship is not to be based on religion, going through the motions or rituals, but a relationship. I can't tell you what your relationship should or would be or look like; that is between you and the Father, and how far you want to go with God. I can say that if you seek Him, you will find Him.

He will, however, place people in your life that will help encourage you in your walk and show you how to build a relationship and a partnership with Him. The Holy Spirit will be your most excellent teacher and advocate. You can get as close to God as you want, or you can keep your distance; one thing for sure is God still loves you and wants to be God in your life, and through you.

Having and maintaining a personal relationship/partnership with God is the most important aspect of your new life.

When you were born again and placed back into a position that's unchangeable, the question that I have for you is what will you do to access all that this position has made available?

The building of your relationship will not happen overnight, as it will take more than just one time to build this relationship. It is a lifelong journey; it's one worth pursuing wholeheartedly. I want to encourage you to keep seeking your Heavenly Father every day. You may be asking, "How do I do this?" It starts with an acknowledgment of His presence and obeying His voice. Pray to Him and let Him know you need Him; talk to Him by saying, "Show me, Jesus, how to be like You and Holy Spirit. Help me with this," while giving Him thanks, worship, and praise in everything. Let what you say and how you communicate with Him come from your heart, spending time in prayer and with the Word. Your relationship is personal and is a two-way relationship.

John 10:10 (NKJV)

> *The thief does not come except to steal, and to kill, and to destroy. I have come that they may have life, and that they may have it more abundantly.*

Think with me for a moment, in the natural, about the process of starting a new relationship.

This example is light when compared to the relationship you can have with the Father.

Imagine you meet someone, and let's say you and that person become friends. You will spend time getting to know him/her by talking to him/her, watching him/her, asking him/her questions, and understanding his/her ways: the reason why he/she does what he/she does. You study and make a note of the person's likes and dislikes. You watch him/her up close and sometimes from afar (meaning you're watching him/her when he/she doesn't know you are watching him/her). You get to know the person's character and his/her level of integrity. You check him/her out to see if the person is trustworthy, dependable, and truthful, and at the same time, he/she is also looking for all those things in you. You will learn the person's motive—why do we want this friendship or relationship? Both parties become transparent.

You talk to the person, and you listen to him/her. Building and maintaining a healthy relationship takes time. I think we too often don't take the time to build strong, lasting relationships, especially with those God has placed in our lives. You show them you care by your actions. You create an intimacy.

Now when I talk about your relationship and partnership with the Almighty, first of all, there is no natural comparison that I could ever give that would measure up to the relationship with our Father.

When you get to know the Father, you are getting to know yourself. He supersedes the requirements of any natural relationship; yet He wants to relate to you in your current state, so He sent Jesus, who can relate to the things we go through and shows us how to live. By showing you how you are in Him, this is done through relationship.

I want to show you two Scriptures that relate to Jesus going through the same things we face today, as well as the love and commitment of the Father to us.

Hebrews 4:15 (NIV)

For we do not have a high priest who is unable to empathize with our weakness, but we have one who has been tempted in every way, just as we are—yet He did not sin.

He has promised to never leave your nor forsake you.

Hebrews 13:5 (AMP)

The middle part of this scripture that says "I WILL NEVER (under any circumstances) DESERT YOU (nor give you up nor leave you without support, nor will I in any degree leave you helpless), NOR WILL I FORSAKE OR LET YOU DOWN OR RELAX MY HOLD ON YOU (assuredly not)!

A real relationship is one built on love. God is saying that no matter what comes or no don't take the time to build strong, lasting relationships, especially with those God has placed in our lives. You show them you care by your actions. You create an intimacy.

Now when I talk about your relationship and partnership with the Almighty, first of all, there is no natural comparison that I could ever give that would measure up to the relationship with our Father.

When you get to know the Father, you are getting to know yourself. He supersedes the requirements of any natural relationship; yet He wants to relate to you in your current state, so He sent Jesus, who can relate to the things we go through and shows us how to live. By showing you how you are in Him, this is done through relationship.

I want to show you two Scriptures that relate to Jesus going through the same things we face today, as well as the love and commitment of the Father to us.

Hebrews 4:15 (NIV)

For we do not have a high priest who is unable to empathize with our weakness, but we have one who has been tempted in every way, just as we are—yet He did not sin.

He has promised to never leave your nor forsake you.

Hebrews 13:5 (AMP)

The middle part of this scripture that says "I WILL NEVER (under any circumstances) DESERT YOU (nor give you up nor leave you without support, nor will I in any degree leave you helpless), NOR WILL I FORSAKE OR LET YOU DOWN OR RELAX MY HOLD ON YOU (assuredly not)!

A real relationship is one built on love. God is saying that no matter what comes or no matter what goes on, He will always be with you and He is in you. This is a promise.

Numbers 23:19 (NLT)

> *God is not a man, so He does not lie.*
>
> *He is not human, so He does not change His mind.*
>
> *Has He ever spoken and failed to act?*
>
> *Has He ever promised and not carried it through?*

The Word says,

Matthew 5:6

> *Blessed are they which do hunger and thirst after righteousness; for they shall be filled.*

And,

James 4:8 (ESV)

Draw near to God, and He will draw near to you. Cleanse your hands, you sinners, and purify your hearts, you double-minded.

My prayer is that this chapter has encouraged you to pursue a real relationship with God the Father, Jesus, and the Holy Spirit, so you may experience God like never before.

Chapter 5

―――∝―――

A New Life

Galatians 2:20

I am crucified with Christ: nevertheless I live; yet not I, but Christ liveth in me: and the life which I now live in the flesh I live by the faith of the son of God, who loved me and gave himself for me.

2 Corinthians 5:17

Therefore, if any man be in Christ, he is a new creature: old things are passed away; behold, all things are become new.

There is much to be said about your new life in Christ Jesus. This chapter will not cover it all, but I hope it will give you a starting place to purse your identity and purpose in Christ. It's a walk of faith; this is a call to action. God is looking for you to partner with Him in the earth.

To help someone else, we must first have our identity right. We must first see ourselves as our Father sees us and know what He has said about us. We do this by renewing our minds. Let's look at the Word.

Romans 12:1-2 (KJV)

> *I beseech you therefore, brethren, by the mercies of God, that ye present your bodies a living sacrifice, holy, acceptable unto God, which is your reasonable service.*
>
> *And be not conformed to this world: but be ye transformed by the renewing of your mind, that ye may prove what is that good, and acceptable, and perfect, will of God.*

Ephesians 2:10 (NLT)

For we are God's masterpiece. He has created us anew in Christ Jesus, so we can do the good things he planned for us long ago.

Ephesians 1:3-8 (NLT)

All praise to God, the Father of our Lord Jesus Christ, who has blessed us with every spiritual blessing in the heavenly realms because we are united with Christ.

Even before He made the world, God loved us and chose us in Christ to be holy and without fault in His eyes.

God decided in advance to adopt us into His own family by bringing us to Himself through Jesus Christ. This is what He wanted to do, and it gave Him great pleasure.

So we praise God for the glorious grace He has poured out on us who belong to His dear Son.

He is so rich in kindness and grace that He purchased our freedom with the blood of His Son and forgave our sins.

He has showered His kindness on us, along with all wisdom and understanding.

Ephesians 1:11 (NLT)

Furthermore, because we are united with Christ, we have received an inheritance from God,[c] for he chose us in advance, and he makes everything work out according to his plan.

Ephesians 1:13-14 (NLT)

And now you Gentiles have also heard the truth, the Good News that God saves you. And when you believed in Christ, he identified you as his own[d] by giving you the Holy Spirit, whom he promised long ago.

The Spirit is God's guarantee He will give us the inheritance He promised and that He has purchased us to be His own people. He did this so we would praise and glorify Him.

Let's recap what we just read.

    You are blessed.

    God loves you.

    You are chosen by God.

    You have been adopted into the family of God as His own.

    You are free.

    You are forgiven.

You have been given all wisdom and understanding.

You have an inheritance.

We must understand that we are in this world, but not of this world (John 17:16, KJV). You may be asking what this means; it means that while we are living in this world, we don't come from this world. We come from God and don't take our orders from this world's system; we walk in dominion and authority. We are children of the Most High God. We have God's DNA.

I am learning that God can use us right where we are, if we are open to Him and allow Him to lead us, prompt us, and empower us through our spirit man, and if we are bold enough to walk by faith and want to do things that will give Him glory.

Your new life gives you the ability and authority to operate just like Christ on the earth.

John 14:12 (NLT)

> *I tell you the truth, anyone who believes in me will do the same works I have done, and even greater works, because I am going to be with the Father.*

Your new life gives you access to the mind of Christ.

Philippians 2:5 (KJV)

> *Let this mind be in you, which was also in Christ Jesus.*

You can think just like Jesus, and you can handle and respond to life's situations just like Christ. When others in the world can't figure out the answer, you have the ability to tap into the mind of Christ through the power of the Holy Spirit and faith. We can operate in this world just like Jesus, just like God Himself. I know this may sound strange to you, but it is your identity.

John 14:26 (AMP)

> *But the Helper (Comforter, Advocate, Intercessor-Counselor, Strengther, Standby), the Holy Spirit, whom the Father will send in My name (in my place, to represent Me and act on my behalf), He will teach you all things. And He will help you remember everything that I have told you.*

What I have shared so far isn't all that is available. There is still so much more. You may be thinking, *Ok, this is great, but how do I access this?* First, by faith, believing, receiving, and knowing that this is all available to you and, most importantly, relying totally on the Holy Spirit to help you walk through your process.

This new life isn't all about the benefits that we have access to, but it is also about showing others God through your life, leading them to Christ and the identity that they have in Him.

Mark 16:15-20 (KJV)

And he said unto them, Go ye into all the world, and preach the gospel to every creature.

He that believeth and is baptized shall be saved; but he that believeth not shall be damned.

And these signs shall follow them that believe; In my name shall they cast out devils; they shall speak with new tongues;

They shall take up serpents; and if they drink any deadly thing, it shall not hurt them; they shall lay hands on the sick, and they shall recover.

So then after the Lord had spoken unto them, he was received up into heaven, and sat on the right hand of God.

And they went forth, and preached every where, the Lord working with them, and confirming the word with signs following. Amen.

I believe that we have our gifts and abilities to help point others to Jesus and to show them who they are. To help someone else, we must first have our identity right. We must first see ourselves as our Father sees us. We do this by renewing our minds. This life isn't about self, but about how many we can help along the way.

A misconception about this walk that I would like to address is that once you become saved, your life will be easy with no trials or tests. This isn't entirely true. We have an adversary, and his job is to accuse us before God. We will have tests and trials, but there will be no need to worry or be thrown off course if we know our identity and, according to the Word, know how to respond. Remember, you are victorious!

1 Peter 5:8-9 (NLT)

Stay alert! Watch out for your great enemy, the devil. He prowls around like a roaring lion, looking for someone to devour.

Stand firm against him, and be strong in your faith. Remember that your family of believers [b] all over the world is going through the same kind of suffering you are.

James 1:2-8 (NLT)

Dear brothers and sisters, [a] when troubles of any kind come your way, consider it an opportunity for great joy.

For you know that when your faith is tested, your endurance has a chance to grow.

So let it grow, for when your endurance is fully developed, you will be perfect and complete, needing nothing.

If you need wisdom, ask our generous God, and he will give it to you. He will not rebuke you for asking.

But when you ask him, be sure that your faith is in God alone. Do not waver, for a person with divided loyalty is as unsettled as a wave of the sea that is blown and tossed by the wind.

Such people should not expect to receive anything from the Lord.

Their loyalty is divided between God and the world, and they are unstable in everything they do.

John 16:33 (KJV)

These things I have spoken unto you, that in me ye might have peace. In the world ye shall have tribulation: but be of good cheer; I have overcome the world.

The Word is clear, and our response is also clear. We must be doers of the Word. We win every time! What helps me is this: I know that God is with me, in me, and for me. If He allowed it, then I believe He checked it out, and He said, "She has all she needs to handle this and be victorious." This gives me the extra confidence I need to go through the test or trial. Every encounter I have with God, I know that He is building something within me that is unshakeable.

Looking back over my journey so far, I see now where the old would try to keep me from changing. Old habits and the old way of thinking would try to keep me on lockdown so that the real me wouldn't come forth. This isn't something that is defeated one time, but I have learned that as I continue to walk with the Lord every day, He helps me to respond the right way. I had to make the decision to do something different.

Do I make every choice right? No, but I do endeavor to live a life that pleases God and lines up with the Word. For example,

He used my mentor to help me to earnestly pray for people who I knew were against me, instead of trying to get even. By His Spirit, He taught me how to really forgive people. For example, I told myself that I forgave my ex-husband, but my actions were saying something different. I went on for months thinking that I had forgiven him. Then it was like the Lord spoke to my spirit and said, "You haven't forgiven him. Look at the way you are treating him and the attitude you get when you talk to him."

This caused me to check my heart toward him and to pray for God's help to forgive him. See, I had a choice: I could have ignored His leading and kept fooling myself into thinking that I had forgiven him, or yield and change. I repented and asked God to help me to forgive him, and today, I truly forgive him. I don't even bring up the past to hurt him or me, and I want the best for him; and I do believe that God will do great things in his life. The Word says:

Mark 11:25 (KJV)

> *And when ye stand praying, forgive, if ye have ought against any: that your Father also which is in heaven may forgive you your trespasses.*

Ephesians 4:32 (KJV)

> *And be ye kind one to another, tenderhearted, forgiving one another, even as God for Christ's sake hath forgiven you.*

Luke 6:28 (KJV)

> *Bless them that curse you, and pray for them which despitefully use you.*

We must not allow anything to come between our relationship with our Heavenly Father. This life is a journey, one that's meant to be enjoyed and filled with good things.

Jeremiah 29:11 (KJV)

For I know the thoughts that I think toward you, saith the Lord, thoughts of peace, and not of evil, to give you an expected end.

Philippians 1:6 (KJV)

Being confident of this very thing, that he which hath begun a good work in you will perform it until the day of Jesus Christ:

Hebrews 12:1-2 (KJV)

Wherefore seeing we also are compassed about with so great a cloud of witnesses, let us lay aside every weight, and the sin which doth so easily beset us, and let us run with patience the race that is set before us,

Looking unto Jesus the author and finisher of our faith; who for the joy that was set before him endured the cross, despising the shame, and is set down at the right hand of the throne of God.

1 Corinthians 2:2 (KJV)

For I determined not to know any thing among you, save Jesus Christ, and him crucified.

Joshua 1:8 (NLT)

Study this book of instruction continually. Meditate on it day and night so you will be sure to obey everything written in it. Only then will you prosper and succeed in all you do.

There is so much that God has for you as a born-again child of God and so many great things that He has already given to you. He has made it possible for you to experience it right here and right now. Search the Scriptures, renew your mind to find out what God says about you, and then allow what He has done and said about you to change the way you see Him, the way you see yourself, and the way you see others.

Prayer of Salvation

(provided by Mt. Gilead Full Gospel Ministries)

Father, I thank you for Your Son, Jesus, and for sending Him to die on the cross for my sins.

I believe in my heart that Jesus died on the cross for my sins, and I believe that You raised Him from the dead on the third day.

Therefore, I confess with my mouth that I am a sinner. I have done wrong and sinned against You and You only. God, I am sorry. Father, forgive me of my sins.

Lord Jesus, come into my heart and wash away all of my sins with Your blood.

I receive You now as my Lord and personal Savior.

Thank you, Lord, for saving me, and right now, I am born again!

Right now, I am a Christian!

Right now, I am saved!

In Jesus's name, AMEN.

Additional Resources to Read for Spiritual Growth

Plug In
   By Bishop Daniel Robertson Jr. (Author)

The Mentor in You
   By Elena Robertson

Cross Factor: The Inherent Benefits of the Blood
   By Apostle Leroy Thompson

The Holy Spirit and His Gifts
   By Kenneth E. Hagin

Spirit Life Training
   By Timothy Jorgensen

www.ingramcontent.com/pod-product-compliance
Ingram Content Group UK Ltd.
Pitfield, Milton Keynes, MK11 3LW, UK
UKHW041948230426
12048UKWH00008B/213